THE RISE OF INTELLIGENT MACHINES

AI in Everyday Life

Najeed Khan

This book is lovingly dedicated to my mother, Prof. Dr. Anisa Basheer Khan, who has been a constant source of inspiration and motivation throughout my life.

This book is lovingly dedicated to my mother, Prof. Dr. Anisa Basheer Khan, who has been a constant source of inspiration and motivation throughout my life.

CONTENTS

Title Page
Dedication
Preface
Prologue
Introduction to Intelligent Machines   1
AI in the Home   7
AI in Personal Assistants   13
AI in Entertainment   19
Future of AI in Daily Life   25
Bibliography   30
About The Author   33
Books By This Author   37

PREFACE

Artificial intelligence (AI) has transitioned from being a subject of speculative fiction to an integral part of our daily lives. From the voice assistants that respond to our questions to the algorithms curating our entertainment, AI is no longer a concept of the future—it is the reality of today. The inspiration for this book, *The Rise of Intelligent Machines: AI in Everyday Life*, stems from the need to understand and appreciate the profound ways in which AI is transforming our world.

The story of AI is not just one of technological progress but of human ingenuity and adaptation. Over the past decades, advancements in machine learning, natural language processing, and robotics have unlocked capabilities once thought impossible. These innovations are reshaping industries, influencing cultures, and redefining what it means to interact with technology. Yet, amidst this rapid transformation, there is a pressing need to demystify AI and explore its implications for individuals, communities, and society at large.

This book is designed to bridge the gap between the technical and the tangible, offering readers a comprehensive look at how AI intersects with everyday experiences. Each chapter delves into a specific domain—from the personalized comforts of smart homes to the creative possibilities in entertainment, and from the productivity enhancements of personal assistants to the ethical dilemmas posed by AI's growing influence. By examining these topics through the lens of research, case studies, and expert insights, this book provides a holistic view of AI's transformative power.

But this is not merely a celebration of technology. As much as AI offers unprecedented opportunities, it also presents significant challenges. Issues of privacy, bias, job displacement, and accountability demand thoughtful consideration and proactive solutions. Throughout the book, I emphasize the importance of responsible AI development and the role of human values in guiding its trajectory. These discussions are crucial as we navigate an increasingly AI-driven world.

As the author of this book, I am driven by a passion for exploring how technology shapes human life. My background in AI research, strategy, and storytelling have allowed me to approach this subject with both technical rigor and an appreciation for its societal implications. It is my hope that this book will not only inform but also inspire readers to engage with AI—to understand its potential, question its impacts, and imagine its future.

Whether you are a technophile, a skeptic, or simply curious about the world of AI, this book invites you to explore the rise of intelligent machines and their role in everyday life. As we stand at the intersection of possibility and responsibility, let us embark on this journey together to uncover what AI means for all of us.

Welcome to *The Rise of Intelligent Machines*.

Najeed Khan

PROLOGUE

The Rise of Intelligent Machines: AI in Everyday Life is a comprehensive exploration of how artificial intelligence (AI) is transforming various aspects of daily existence. This book delves into the profound impact of AI across multiple domains, offering readers a blend of historical perspective, current applications, and future possibilities.

The book opens with an introduction to intelligent machines, tracing the evolution of AI from its conceptual beginnings to its modern-day applications. Drawing on insights from thinkers like Nick Bostrom and Pedro Domingos, the first chapter provides a foundational understanding of AI technologies, their mechanisms, and their implications for humanity.

Subsequent chapters focus on specific areas where AI has already made significant inroads:

- **AI in the Home:** From smart speakers to automated home systems, this chapter discusses how AI enhances convenience, safety, and efficiency in domestic settings. It examines the rapid adoption of smart home technologies, supported by insights from researchers like Greg Bell and industry reports by Voicebot.ai.

- **AI in Personal Assistants:** Personal assistants such as Siri, Alexa, and Google Assistant have revolutionized productivity and communication. This chapter explores the technological underpinnings and societal impact of these tools, referencing works by Kai-Fu Lee and Timothy Bailey.

- **AI in Entertainment:** AI has redefined how we consume and create entertainment. From personalized recommendations to AI-driven content creation, this chapter highlights the transformative role of AI in shaping modern media and empathic technologies, drawing on analyses by Adam Greenfield and Andrew McStay.

The book's final chapter projects into the future of AI in daily life. It examines potential advancements in smart cities, healthcare, education, and creativity while addressing ethical challenges such as privacy, bias, and economic disruption. Insights from Max Tegmark's *Life 3.0* and Yuval Noah Harari's *21 Lessons for the 21st Century* provide a roadmap for navigating the opportunities and risks of AI integration.

Throughout the book, optimism is balanced with caution, emphasizing the need for responsible development and governance of AI systems. With engaging narratives and thoughtful analyses, *The Rise of Intelligent Machines* offers readers a deep understanding of AI's role in shaping the present and the future, equipping them to participate in informed discussions about this transformative technology.

INTRODUCTION TO INTELLIGENT MACHINES

The journey of intelligent machines, from rudimentary automata to the sophisticated systems that permeate our lives today, marks one of humanity's most remarkable achievements. In the past few decades, the rise of artificial intelligence (AI) has transformed industries, reshaped societies, and redefined what it means to be human in an increasingly digital age. This chapter explores the foundations of intelligent machines, tracing their evolution, current applications, and the profound questions they pose for our collective future.

The Evolution of Intelligence in Machines

The idea of creating intelligent machines predates modern computing. Visionaries like Charles Babbage and Ada Lovelace conceptualized mechanical "thinking" devices in the 19th century. However, the field of AI truly began to take shape in the mid-20th century with pioneers such as Alan Turing, whose famous Turing Test provided a framework for evaluating machine intelligence. Since then, the development of AI has been fueled by advances in computing power, algorithms, and data availability.

Nick Bostrom, in his seminal work *Superintelligence: Paths, Dangers, Strategies*, emphasizes the transformative potential of AI. He discusses how machines that surpass human intelligence in specific domains could lead to unprecedented opportunities and risks. Bostrom's analysis underscores the importance of guiding the development of intelligent systems to ensure they align with human values and objectives.

Foundations of Intelligent Machines

Intelligent machines rely on several core technologies:

1. **Machine Learning (ML):** As Pedro Domingos explains in *The Master Algorithm*, machine learning is the science of getting computers to learn from data. ML systems identify patterns and make predictions, often outperforming humans in tasks such as image recognition and language translation.
2. **Natural Language Processing (NLP):** NLP enables machines to understand and generate human language. Applications like chatbots and virtual assistants, such as Siri and Alexa, exemplify the progress in this area.
3. **Computer Vision:** This technology allows machines to interpret visual data, enabling applications ranging from facial recognition to autonomous vehicles.
4. **Robotics:** By combining AI with physical systems, robotics has revolutionized industries such as manufacturing, healthcare, and logistics.

AI in Everyday Life

Erik Brynjolfsson and Andrew McAfee's *The Second Machine*

Age highlights how intelligent machines are reshaping work and society. From personalized recommendations on streaming platforms to sophisticated fraud detection systems in banking, AI is embedded in countless aspects of modern life. Key examples include:

- **Healthcare:** AI-driven diagnostic tools analyze medical images with accuracy comparable to human experts. Machine learning models are used to predict patient outcomes and optimize treatment plans.
- **Transportation:** Autonomous vehicles leverage AI to navigate complex environments, promising safer and more efficient transportation systems.
- **Education:** Intelligent tutoring systems adapt to individual learning styles, enhancing educational outcomes.
- **Business:** AI optimizes supply chains, enhances customer experiences, and automates repetitive tasks, boosting productivity.

Opportunities and Challenges

The integration of intelligent machines into daily life brings significant benefits but also poses challenges. As Bostrom warns, the advent of superintelligent systems could lead to scenarios where human oversight becomes difficult, raising concerns about ethical decision-making and societal impact. Similarly, Brynjolfsson and McAfee point to the risk of economic displacement as machines outperform humans in various jobs.

Addressing these challenges requires interdisciplinary collaboration and proactive policy-making. Ensuring fairness, transparency, and accountability in AI systems is crucial to building public trust. Furthermore, fostering global cooperation can mitigate risks associated with AI misuse and promote equitable access to its benefits.

The Road Ahead

As we stand at the cusp of a new era, the potential of intelligent machines remains boundless. Guided by insights from thought leaders like Bostrom, Domingos, and Brynjolfsson, we can harness AI to address humanity's greatest challenges—from climate change to healthcare disparities. At the same time, vigilance and responsibility are paramount to ensure that this powerful technology serves as a force for good.

This book will delve deeper into the applications, implications, and ethical dimensions of intelligent machines. By understanding their origins and trajectory, we can better navigate the complexities of an AI-driven future and unlock the full potential of these transformative technologies.

References

1. Bostrom, N. (2014). *Superintelligence: Paths, Dangers, Strategies*. Oxford University Press.
2. Domingos, P. (2015). *The Master Algorithm: How the Quest for the Ultimate Learning Machine Will Remake Our World*. Basic Books.
3. Brynjolfsson, E., & McAfee, A. (2014). *The Second Machine Age: Work, Progress, and Prosperity in a Time of Brilliant Technologies*. W.W. Norton & Company.

THE RISE OF INTELLIGENT MACHINES

NAJEED KHAN

AI IN THE HOME

The rise of artificial intelligence (AI) in the home has transformed the way we live, work, and interact within our personal spaces. Once the realm of science fiction, the concept of a "smart home" powered by AI is now a reality, enhancing convenience, security, and efficiency. This chapter explores the integration of AI into the home, examining its applications, benefits, and the challenges of widespread adoption.

The Foundations of Smart Homes

The modern smart home is built on a network of connected devices, sensors, and software that enable automation and intelligent decision-making. Central to this ecosystem are AI-driven systems that learn user preferences and adapt to individual needs. Graham Bell's *Smart Home Systems* provides a comprehensive overview of how these technologies converge to create interconnected environments that simplify everyday tasks and improve quality of life.

Voice Assistants: The Gateway to AI in the Home

Voice-activated assistants, such as Amazon Alexa, Google

Assistant, and Apple's Siri, are among the most visible and widely adopted applications of AI in the home. According to Bret Kinsella's *Voicebot Report: Smart Speaker Consumer Adoption Report*, the adoption of smart speakers has grown exponentially in recent years, with millions of households relying on them for tasks like:

- Controlling smart home devices (e.g., lighting, thermostats, and appliances).
- Managing schedules and reminders.
- Providing hands-free access to information and entertainment.

Voice assistants exemplify the power of natural language processing (NLP) and machine learning to create seamless and intuitive user experiences. As these systems continue to evolve, their capabilities expand to include more complex interactions and personalized services.

Key Applications of AI in the Home

AI's integration into the home extends beyond voice assistants. Michael Hargrave's *The Smart Home Manual* outlines a variety of AI-driven technologies designed to enhance home life, including:

1. **Energy Management:** Smart thermostats like Nest and Ecobee use machine learning to optimize energy usage, reducing costs and environmental impact.
2. **Home Security:** AI-powered surveillance cameras and alarm systems, such as Ring and Arlo, offer features like facial recognition, motion detection, and real-time alerts to enhance safety.

3. **Entertainment:** AI is embedded in streaming platforms, such as Netflix and Spotify, to deliver personalized content recommendations, creating a more engaging entertainment experience.
4. **Health and Wellness:** AI-enabled devices, such as sleep trackers and fitness wearables, provide insights into physical activity, sleep patterns, and overall health, empowering users to make informed lifestyle decisions.
5. **Appliances:** AI integration in household appliances, such as smart refrigerators and robotic vacuum cleaners, simplifies daily chores and improves efficiency.

Benefits of AI in the Home

The adoption of AI in the home offers numerous advantages, including:

- **Convenience:** Automation of routine tasks frees up time for other activities.
- **Personalization:** AI learns from user behavior to deliver tailored experiences.
- **Energy Efficiency:** Intelligent energy management systems reduce waste and lower utility bills.
- **Enhanced Security:** Real-time monitoring and alerts improve home safety.

Challenges and Considerations

Despite its benefits, the implementation of AI in the home presents challenges. Hargrave highlights concerns about privacy and data security, as smart home devices often collect and transmit sensitive information. Ensuring robust encryption and transparent data policies is critical to addressing these issues.

Additionally, Kinsella's research points to the need for greater interoperability among devices from different manufacturers. Standardized protocols and frameworks could streamline integration and enhance user experience.

The Future of AI in the Home

As AI technologies continue to advance, the potential for smarter, more interconnected homes will expand. Innovations such as predictive maintenance for appliances, AI-driven elder care solutions, and augmented reality interfaces are poised to redefine home living. However, realizing this potential requires careful consideration of ethical, societal, and technical challenges.

The next chapter will explore AI's role in personal assistants, highlighting its transformative impact in improving personal efficiency. By understanding AI's capabilities and limitations in the home, we can better navigate its broader implications in everyday life.

References

1. Kinsella, B. (2018). *Voicebot Report: Smart Speaker Consumer Adoption Report*. Voicebot.ai.
2. Bell, G. (2017). *Smart Home Systems*. Springer.
3. Hargrave, M. (2018). *The Smart Home Manual: How to Automate Your Home to Keep Your Family Entertained, Comfortable, and Safe*. CreateSpace Independent Publishing Platform.

THE RISE OF INTELLIGENT MACHINES

NAJEED KHAN

AI IN PERSONAL ASSISTANTS

The advent of AI-powered personal assistants has revolutionized how individuals manage their daily lives, making complex tasks simpler and more efficient. These systems, fueled by advances in artificial intelligence, machine learning, and natural language processing, have become indispensable tools for personal and professional productivity. This chapter explores the role of AI in personal assistants, their capabilities, the challenges they present, and their potential to reshape human-AI interaction.

The Evolution of Personal Assistants

AI-driven personal assistants, such as Siri, Google Assistant, and Alexa, have their roots in early speech recognition and natural language processing technologies. Over time, these systems have evolved into sophisticated platforms capable of understanding context, learning user preferences, and executing complex tasks.

Kai-Fu Lee's *AI Superpowers* underscores the role of competitive innovation between tech hubs like Silicon Valley and China in driving the development of AI technologies. He highlights how companies like Apple, Google, and Baidu have invested heavily in AI research to create personal assistants that are more intuitive and responsive, catering to diverse user needs worldwide.

Capabilities of AI Personal Assistants

AI personal assistants offer a wide range of functionalities that enhance productivity, convenience, and accessibility. These include:

1. **Task Management:** AI assistants can schedule appointments, set reminders, and manage to-do lists, streamlining daily routines.
2. **Information Retrieval:** By leveraging internet-connected databases, these systems provide instant answers to user queries, ranging from weather updates to complex research questions.
3. **Communication:** Personal assistants facilitate hands-free communication by sending messages, making calls, and managing emails.
4. **Smart Home Integration:** AI assistants can control connected home devices, such as lighting, security systems, and appliances, enhancing home automation.
5. **E-commerce Support:** They assist users in online shopping, from placing orders to tracking deliveries.
6. **Multilingual Support:** Many personal assistants offer translation services, breaking down language barriers.

Opportunities and Benefits

The integration of AI in personal assistants has unlocked numerous opportunities. As Timothy Bailey notes in *The AI-Powered Entrepreneur*, these systems enable professionals to focus on high-value tasks by automating mundane activities. Entrepreneurs, for instance, can use AI assistants to handle scheduling, customer communication, and data analysis, allowing them to scale their operations efficiently.

Moreover, personal assistants promote accessibility for individuals with disabilities. Voice-activated systems provide an inclusive interface for those who face challenges with traditional input methods, empowering greater independence and participation.

Challenges and Ethical Considerations

Despite their benefits, AI personal assistants also pose significant challenges. M. U. Scherer's analysis in *Regulating Artificial Intelligence Systems* emphasizes the risks associated with privacy and data security. Since these systems often rely on continuous data collection to improve their services, they can inadvertently expose sensitive information to misuse or unauthorized access.

Other challenges include:

- **Bias and Fairness:** Personal assistants may exhibit biases based on the datasets they are trained on, potentially reinforcing stereotypes.
- **Transparency:** The decision-making processes of AI systems are often opaque, raising concerns about accountability and trust.
- **Over-Reliance:** As users become more dependent on personal assistants, there is a risk of diminishing critical thinking and problem-solving skills.

The Future of AI Personal Assistants

The future of AI personal assistants lies in enhanced personalization, emotional intelligence, and proactive decision-making. Advances in contextual awareness and emotional AI will allow these systems to better understand user sentiments and respond empathetically, creating more natural and human-like interactions.

Kai-Fu Lee's vision of an AI-driven world highlights the role of competition and collaboration in shaping the next generation of personal assistants. For example, integrating advanced AI with augmented reality (AR) could lead to immersive virtual assistants that provide on-the-go guidance and support in both personal and professional settings.

Conclusion

AI personal assistants represent a significant milestone in the journey toward intelligent machines. By leveraging their capabilities, individuals can achieve greater efficiency and accessibility in their daily lives. However, addressing ethical concerns and technical limitations is essential to ensuring these systems serve humanity responsibly. The next chapter will explore AI's role in reshaping entertainment, further demonstrating its transformative impact on everyday life.

References

1. Scherer, M. U. (2016). *Regulating Artificial Intelligence Systems: Risks, Challenges, Competencies, and Strategies.* Harvard Journal of Law & Technology, 29(2), 353-400.

2. Lee, K-F. (2018). *AI Superpowers: China, Silicon Valley, and the New World Order.* Houghton Mifflin Harcourt.

3. Bailey, T. (2019). *The AI-Powered Entrepreneur: Leveraging AI Tools to Grow Your Business.* Independently published.

NAJEED KHAN

AI IN ENTERTAINMENT

The entertainment industry has undergone a profound transformation with the integration of artificial intelligence (AI). From personalized recommendations to content creation, AI technologies are reshaping how we consume, create, and engage with entertainment. This chapter explores the role of AI in entertainment, its applications, and its impact on audiences and creators alike.

The Integration of AI into Entertainment

Entertainment has always been at the forefront of adopting new technologies to captivate audiences. With the rise of AI, entertainment platforms and creators are leveraging machine learning, natural language processing, and emotional AI to deliver more immersive and tailored experiences. As Adam Greenfield explains in *Radical Technologies*, AI is not just a tool but a transformative force that influences the design and delivery of everyday life, including entertainment.

AI in Content Recommendation Systems

One of the most prominent applications of AI in entertainment is personalized content recommendation. Streaming platforms like Netflix, Spotify, and YouTube rely on AI algorithms to analyze user preferences and suggest content tailored to individual tastes. Alex Hern's article, *How Netflix is Using AI to Conquer the World*, highlights how Netflix's AI-driven recommendation engine accounts for the majority of user engagement, ensuring viewers spend more time watching and less time searching.

Key components of recommendation systems include:

1. **Data Analysis:** AI systems analyze viewing habits, ratings, and search histories to predict what users will enjoy.

2. **Collaborative Filtering:** This approach identifies patterns by comparing users with similar preferences.

3. **Content-Based Filtering:** AI recommends content based on the attributes of previously consumed media.

By continually refining these algorithms, platforms can offer highly engaging and personalized experiences, driving user retention and satisfaction.

AI in Content Creation

AI is no longer just a tool for curation; it has become an active participant in content creation. Advances in generative AI have enabled the development of:

- **Scriptwriting and Storytelling:** AI tools like OpenAI's ChatGPT can assist in drafting scripts, generating plot ideas, and creating dialogue.

- **Music Composition:** AI-powered platforms like AIVA and Amper Music compose original music tailored to specific moods or themes.

- **Visual Effects and Animation:** AI accelerates rendering processes and enhances visual effects, allowing creators to produce stunning visuals more efficiently.

Greenfield's analysis emphasizes how AI disrupts traditional creative processes, enabling new forms of expression while raising questions about authorship and creativity.

Emotional AI and Empathic Media

Andrew McStay's *Emotional AI: The Rise of Empathic Media* introduces the concept of AI systems that understand and respond to human emotions. In entertainment, emotional AI enhances user experiences by adapting content based on real-time emotional feedback. Examples include:

- **Interactive Games:** AI-driven characters in video games respond dynamically to player emotions, creating more immersive narratives.
- **Streaming Platforms:** Emotional AI adjusts recommendations or playback settings to align with a viewer's mood.
- **Live Performances:** AI technologies analyze audience reactions to optimize lighting, sound, and performance elements in real time.

These empathic systems create a deeper connection between audiences and media, offering personalized and emotionally resonant experiences.

Challenges and Ethical Considerations

While AI enriches entertainment, it also introduces challenges. Greenfield warns of the risks of over-optimization, where recommendation systems prioritize engagement over diversity, leading to echo chambers and reduced exposure to varied content. Additionally, McStay raises ethical concerns about emotional AI, such as privacy violations and the commodification of human emotions.

Other challenges include:

- **Authenticity:** As AI-generated content becomes indistinguishable from human-created work, audiences may struggle to discern authenticity.
- **Bias in Algorithms:** AI systems can perpetuate biases present in training data, affecting representation and fairness.
- **Impact on Creative Jobs:** Automation in content creation could disrupt traditional roles in the entertainment industry.

The Future of AI in Entertainment

The future of AI in entertainment is boundless, with emerging technologies poised to revolutionize the industry further. Greenfield envisions a world where AI collaborates seamlessly with human creators, enhancing creativity rather than replacing it. Innovations such as virtual reality (VR), augmented reality

(AR), and holographic media will blur the lines between physical and digital experiences, offering unprecedented levels of immersion.

Additionally, the integration of emotional AI will enable entertainment that adapts not just to individual preferences but to the nuances of human emotion, creating truly empathic media experiences.

Conclusion

AI has become an integral part of the entertainment ecosystem, redefining how content is created, consumed, and experienced. While it offers exciting opportunities for innovation and personalization, it also demands careful consideration of ethical and societal implications. As we explore AI's role in other industries, its impact on entertainment serves as a testament to its transformative potential in everyday life.

References

1. Greenfield, A. (2018). *Radical Technologies: The Design of Everyday Life*. Verso.
2. Hern, A. (2017). *How Netflix is Using AI to Conquer the World*. The Guardian.
3. McStay, A. (2018). *Emotional AI: The Rise of Empathic Media*. Sage Publications.

NAJEED KHAN

FUTURE OF AI IN DAILY LIFE

As artificial intelligence (AI) continues to advance, its potential to reshape daily life is vast and transformative. From personalized services to complex decision-making, AI's future applications will redefine how we interact with technology, society, and each other. This chapter explores the trajectory of AI in everyday life, drawing on insights from leading thinkers to anticipate the opportunities and challenges that lie ahead.

AI and the Evolution of Expertise

The integration of AI into professional and personal domains is already altering the role of human expertise. In *The Future of the Professions*, Richard and Daniel Susskind argue that AI will increasingly take over tasks traditionally performed by experts, from diagnosing diseases to providing legal advice. This shift will democratize access to services, enabling individuals to benefit from high-quality expertise without requiring face-to-face interactions.

For example:

- **Healthcare:** AI-powered diagnostic tools will allow individuals to monitor their health in real-time, identifying potential issues before they become serious.

- **Education:** Personalized learning platforms, driven by AI, will tailor content to each student's needs, enhancing educational outcomes and accessibility.
- **Finance:** Automated financial advisors will provide personalized investment strategies, helping people manage their finances with greater precision.

While these changes promise increased efficiency and accessibility, they also raise questions about the role of human professionals and the skills required to remain relevant in an AI-driven world.

Life in the Age of AI

Max Tegmark's *Life 3.0* envisions a future where AI systems evolve beyond current capabilities, becoming active participants in shaping human society. This vision includes:

1. **Enhanced Personalization:** AI will predict and adapt to individual needs, creating seamless experiences across all aspects of life. From recommending meals to optimizing daily schedules, AI will anticipate and address user preferences.
2. **Smart Cities:** Urban areas will leverage AI for efficient resource management, including energy consumption, transportation, and waste reduction. Autonomous vehicles and intelligent traffic systems will reduce congestion and environmental impact.
3. **Augmented Creativity:** AI tools will collaborate with humans in creative endeavors, from composing music to designing products, enabling unprecedented innovation.

However, Tegmark cautions against complacency, highlighting

the need for governance frameworks to ensure that AI systems align with human values and objectives.

The Ethical Landscape

As AI becomes more integrated into daily life, ethical considerations will grow increasingly urgent. Yuval Noah Harari's *21 Lessons for the 21st Century* emphasizes the need to address questions of privacy, inequality, and control. Key concerns include:

- **Privacy:** With AI systems constantly collecting data, maintaining individual privacy will be a significant challenge. Transparent policies and robust encryption will be essential to safeguard personal information.
- **Bias and Fairness:** AI algorithms are only as unbiased as the data they are trained on. Ensuring fairness in AI systems will require ongoing scrutiny and diverse datasets.
- **Economic Disruption:** Automation will likely displace jobs, necessitating new approaches to education, job creation, and social safety nets.

Harari advocates for proactive global cooperation to address these challenges, emphasizing the need for shared ethical standards and regulatory frameworks.

Opportunities and Challenges

The future of AI in daily life presents immense opportunities, such as:

- **Improved Quality of Life:** AI-driven solutions will enhance convenience, safety, and productivity.
- **Empowerment:** AI will provide tools that amplify human capabilities, enabling people to achieve more with fewer resources.

However, challenges remain, including:

- **Digital Divide:** Ensuring equitable access to AI technologies will be crucial to prevent widening social inequalities.
- **Over-Reliance:** Dependence on AI systems may erode critical thinking and problem-solving skills.
- **Control and Accountability:** Determining who is responsible for AI-driven decisions will be a complex issue in both legal and ethical contexts.

A Vision for the Future

The long-term success of AI in daily life will depend on how effectively humanity navigates its integration. Tegmark and Harari both stress the importance of aligning AI development with human values, fostering collaboration between technologists, policymakers, and society at large.

Key steps include:

- **Education:** Equipping individuals with the skills to thrive in an AI-driven world, including digital literacy and ethical awareness.
- **Collaboration:** Promoting interdisciplinary research to

address the multifaceted implications of AI.

- **Regulation:** Developing policies that balance innovation with accountability, ensuring AI serves the public good.

Conclusion

The future of AI in daily life holds unparalleled promise and profound challenges. By embracing AI's potential while addressing its risks, society can harness this technology to create a more equitable, innovative, and sustainable world.

References

1. Susskind, R., & Susskind, D. (2015). *The Future of the Professions: How Technology Will Transform the Work of Human Experts*. Oxford University Press.
2. Tegmark, M. (2017). *Life 3.0: Being Human in the Age of Artificial Intelligence*. Knopf.
3. Harari, Y. N. (2018). *21 Lessons for the 21st Century*. Spiegel & Grau.

BIBLIOGRAPHY

1. Bailey, T. (2019). *The AI-Powered Entrepreneur: Leveraging AI Tools to Grow Your Business*. Independently published.

2. Bell, G. (2017). *Smart Home Systems*. Springer.

3. Bostrom, N. (2014). *Superintelligence: Paths, Dangers, Strategies*. Oxford University Press.

4. Brynjolfsson, E., & McAfee, A. (2014). *The Second Machine Age: Work, Progress, and Prosperity in a Time of Brilliant Technologies*. W.W. Norton & Company.

5. Domingos, P. (2015). *The Master Algorithm: How the Quest for the Ultimate Learning Machine Will Remake Our World*. Basic Books.

6. Greenfield, A. (2018). *Radical Technologies: The Design of Everyday Life*. Verso.

7. Harari, Y. N. (2018). *21 Lessons for the 21st Century*. Spiegel & Grau.

8. Hargrave, M. (2018). *The Smart Home Manual: How to Automate Your Home to Keep Your Family Entertained, Comfortable, and Safe*. CreateSpace Independent Publishing Platform.

9. Hern, A. (2017). *How Netflix is Using AI to Conquer the World*. The Guardian.

10. Kinsella, B. (2018). *Voicebot Report: Smart Speaker Consumer*

Adoption Report.

ABOUT THE AUTHOR

Najeed Khan

Najeed Khan is a strategic business leader and technology expert with over two decades of experience shaping the intersection of business strategy and emerging technologies. As a trusted advisor to C-suite executives at leading technology companies, he has pioneered approaches to market analysis, strategic planning, and organizational transformation that bridge the gap between technical innovation and business value.

Drawing from his extensive background in telecom, cloud computing, and artificial intelligence, Khan brings a unique perspective to the challenges facing modern enterprises. His expertise spans wireless technology, hyperscaler cloud computing, edge computing, and fintech, complemented by a deep understanding of how these technologies reshape business landscapes.

A recognized thought leader in the autonomous economy, Khan frequently contributes to industry discussions and has served as a panel speaker at prestigious technology forums. His insights are shaped by years of experience developing high-performance teams and driving strategic initiatives across global organizations.

Khan holds particular expertise in market segmentation analysis, business model development, and strategic planning, with a proven track record of translating complex technical concepts into actionable business strategies. His approach combines rigorous analytical thinking with practical business acumen, making him a valued voice in discussions about technology's role in shaping enterprise strategy.

Khan holds an MBA from NYU Stern School of Business and a B.E. (Honors) in Electrical and Electronics Engineering from Birla Institute of Technology and Science, Pilani. This combination of technical education and business training has shaped his unique approach to technology strategy, making him a distinctive voice in discussions about the future of enterprise technology and digital transformation.

BOOKS BY THIS AUTHOR

Applications Of Artificial Intelligence

https://www.amazon.com/dp/B0DQW1MJP7

A boxset series on the applications of artificial intelligence to various industries. Each book dives into a particular industry, the applications of artificial intelligence to that industry, expanding on a few applications, the benefits and challenges for the adoption of artificial intelligence, and the future directions within that industry.

www.ingramcontent.com/pod-product-compliance
Lightning Source LLC
Chambersburg PA
CBHW040242220526
45473CB00001B/339